CHICKEN & BISCUITS

BY DOUGLAS LYONS

DRAMATISTS
PLAY SERVICE
INC.

CHICKEN & BISCUITS
Copyright © 2022, Douglas Lyons

All Rights Reserved

CHICKEN & BISCUITS is fully protected under the copyright laws of the United States of America, and of all countries covered by the International Copyright Union (including the Dominion of Canada and the rest of the British Commonwealth), and of all countries covered by the Pan-American Copyright Convention, the Universal Copyright Convention, the Berne Convention, and of all countries with which the United States has reciprocal copyright relations. No part of this publication may be reproduced in any form by any means (electronic, mechanical, photocopying, recording, or otherwise), or stored in any retrieval system in any way (electronic or mechanical) without written permission of the publisher.

The stock and amateur stage performance rights throughout the world for CHICKEN & BISCUITS are controlled exclusively by Dramatists Play Service, 440 Park Avenue South, New York, NY 10016. **No professional or nonprofessional performance of the Play may be given without obtaining in advance the written permission of Dramatists Play Service and paying the requisite fee.**

All other rights, including without limitation motion picture, recitation, lecturing, public reading, radio broadcasting, television, video or sound recording, and the rights of translation into foreign languages are strictly reserved.

Inquiries concerning all other rights should be addressed to William Morris Endeavor Entertainment, LLC, 11 Madison Avenue, 18th floor, New York, NY 10010. Attn: Michael Finkle.

NOTE ON BILLING

Anyone receiving permission to produce CHICKEN & BISCUITS is required to give credit to the Author(s) as sole and exclusive Author(s) of the Play on the title page of all programs distributed in connection with performances of the Play and in all instances in which the title of the Play appears, including printed or digital materials for advertising, publicizing or otherwise exploiting the Play and/or a production thereof. Please see your production license for font size and typeface requirements.

Be advised that there may be additional credits required in all programs and promotional material. Such language will be listed under the "Additional Billing" section of production licenses. It is the licensee's responsibility to ensure any and all required billing is included in the requisite places, per the terms of the license.

SPECIAL NOTE ON SONGS/RECORDINGS

Dramatists Play Service neither holds the rights to nor grants permission to use any songs or recordings mentioned in the Play. Permission for performances of copyrighted songs, arrangements or recordings mentioned in this Play is not included in our license agreement. The permission of the copyright owner(s) must be obtained for any such use. For any songs and/or recordings mentioned in the Play, other songs, arrangements, or recordings may be substituted provided permission from the copyright owner(s) of such songs, arrangements or recordings is obtained; or songs, arrangements or recordings in the public domain may be substituted.

This play is dedicated to Velma and Tilden Lyons, who raised me to love hard and to laugh harder. And to the women of my family: Edna, Annie Mae, Mer, Ny, Brenda, Sheree, Mona, Gloria, Barbara, Denise, Deborah, Connie, Zarah, Jazz, Monique, Aniya, Zariah, Cynthia, Taylor, Ruby, Becky, Marvella, DAndria, Jet, Lilli, Kendra, Stacy, Lyn, Hester, Tammy, Tamia, Teresa, Jameka, Marie Baker, and Shawn. And the sweet and fashionable Gaynl (Pringle) Roberts. All of your wit and spirit inspired this script. Thank you.

CHICKEN & BISCUITS received its launch production at Queens Theatre (Taryn Sacramone, Executive Director), Queens, New York, on February 28, 2020. It was directed by Zhailon Levingston, the scenic design was by Nate Bertone, the costume design was by Heather McDevitt Barton, the lighting design was by Adam Honoré, the sound design was by Chris Darbassie, and the production stage manager was Rachel Denise April. The cast was as follows:

BANEATTA MABRY .... Jennifer Fouché
REGINALD MABRY .... Robert G. McKay
KENNY MABRY .... Josh Adam Ramos
LOGAN LEIBOWITZ .... Brendan Ellis
BEVERLY JENKINS .... Ebony Marshall-Oliver
LA'TRICE FRANKLIN .... Aigner Mizzelle
SIMONE MABRY .... Alana Raquel Bowers
BRIANNA JENKINS .... Ashanti J'Aria

CHICKEN & BISCUITS was originally produced on Broadway by Pamela Ross, Hunter Arnold, E. Clayton Cornelious, Leah Michalos, Kayla Greenspan, Priyanka Chopra Jonas, Nick Jonas, Mapleseed Productions, Curt Cronin, John Joseph, John Paterakis, and Invisible Wall Productions/Blaine Hopkins at the Circle in the Square Theatre on October 10, 2021. It was directed by Zhailon Levingston, the scenic design was by Lawrence E. Moten III, the costume design was by Dede Ayite, the lighting design was by Adam Honoré, the sound design was by Twi McCallum, the original music was by Michael O. Mitchell, and the production stage manager was lark hackshaw. The cast was as follows:

BANEATTA MABRY .... Cleo King
REGINALD MABRY .... Norm Lewis
KENNY MABRY .... Devere Rogers
LOGAN LEIBOWITZ .... Michael Urie
BEVERLY JENKINS .... Ebony Marshall-Oliver
LA'TRICE FRANKLIN .... Aigner Mizzelle
SIMONE MABRY .... Alana Raquel Bowers
BRIANNA JENKINS .... NaTasha Yvette Williams
UNDERSTUDIES .... Dean Acree (KENNY),
Jennifer Fouché (BANEATTA/BEVERLY/BRIANNA),
Michael Genet (REGINALD), Miles G. Jackson (LOGAN),
Camille Upshaw (SIMONE/LA'TRICE)

CHARACTERS

BANEATTA MABRY—An upstanding and stern Christian woman. Mother to Kenny and Simone, and wife to Reginald. She's overbearingly full of love, but quite uptight and stubborn in her religious ways. Late 40s–mid 50s, African American.

REGINALD MABRY—Baneatta's faithful husband and the new pastor of their home church. He's the peacemaker of the family. Reginald is a ball of love with a side of corny dad jokes. 50s, African American.

KENNY MABRY—Baneatta and Reginald's youngest child. He's proudly queer, but cowers in the presence of his mother. Kenny bites when he needs to, but at the end of the day he just wants to be loved. Mid–late 20s, African American.

LOGAN LEIBOWITZ—Kenny's neurotic and dramatic Jewish boyfriend of four years. He often spins himself into a tizzy, but always wants to be there for Kenny. Logan's weed pen is his crutch for tough times. Mid–late 20s, white.

BEVERLY JENKINS—Baneatta's younger sister. The "fun aunt" who's always in a push-up bra. But don't mistake her vibrance for incompetence. She's a savage, "classy," not so boujee, but definitely ratchet when necessary. Early 40s–50s, African American.

LA'TRICE FRANKLIN—Beverly's daughter. She's nosy, loud, and in everyone's business but her own. When not on her phone, she shows love—but in her own Gen Z way. Sarcasm is her love language. 15, African American.

SIMONE MABRY—Kenny's older sister and Baneatta's favorite. She followed the "right path." Though pulled, she can be shady. While fierce on the exterior, Simone is internally wounded from a recent failed engagement. 30s, African American.

BRIANNA JENKINS—Baneatta and Beverly's half sister through an affair. She didn't know her father, but has come to his funeral to gather more details on him. She's sweet, vulnerable, and collected. Early 40s–50s, African American.

SETTING

Now. St. Luke's Church. New Haven, CT.
Bernard Jenkins's funeral.

NOTES

(—) means the next line comes in quickly thereafter.

(/) means the next line is overlapped at the end of the previous line.

Chicken & Biscuits works when eight vibrant personalities collectively create a family unit before our very eyes. The play lands best when the audience can feel the love that was created in the rehearsal room, so have fun! All gender identities should always be considered to be a part of the family.

The fun of *Chicken and Biscuits* will sometimes allow the audience to overtake the show, encouraging an urge to ham up behavior for laughs. Please resist this holy temptation and keep the family centered and honest, trusting that the text will illuminate the comedy.

"The one thing I feel is lacking in Hollywood today is an understanding of the beauty, the power, the sexuality, the uniqueness, the humor of being a regular Black woman."

—Viola Davis

CHICKEN & BISCUITS

Lights rise on Baneatta Mabry. She sings the hymn "No, Not One" while applying makeup in her living room.

BANEATTA.
JESUS KNOWS ALL ABOUT OUR STRUGGLES
HE WILL GUIDE 'TIL THE DAY IS DONE.

THERE'S NOT A FRIEND LIKE THE LOWLY JESUS
NO NOT ONE, NO NOT ONE.
She notices the clock, they're late.
(Calling.) REGINALD EDWARD MABRY, hurry it up. We are late, and you know I hate being the last *Christian* in the building. *(Beat.)* Reggie!

Baneatta sighs and begins to pray. She paces as she prays.

Lord…please give me your strength on today. Bless me with Your patience to deal with my family, for they know not what they do. Lord, help me keep my eyeballs rolled forward, as they have a tendency to roll backwards around foolishness. And *Lord*, keep me from strangling my baby sister, no matter how much she tests me. For You and I both know…she'll try it. Keep all things unlike You at bay. *(Beat.)* May Daddy's service go as smoothly as Mama's did. I know he's finally resting in Your precious arms, tumor-free. Guide me through today like only *You* can. In Your righteous name, I pray. Ame—

Her cell phone rings. Baneatta doesn't recognize the number. Cautiously she answers, putting on her politest voice.

Hello? Yes, this is Baneatta. Who am I speaking with? *(Beat.)* How did you get this number? *(Beat.)* No-no-no, I told you if you called me again we'd have a serious problem, and I meant it. *(Beat.)* I DON'T CARE! If you dare show your face at my father's service, I'll—

REGINALD. What's all the commotion, woman?

> *Reginald enters, futzing with his tie. Baneatta furiously hangs up.*

Who was that?

BANEATTA. Oh nobody, just a dern bill collector. You know how they press you 'til you snap on'em. What took you so long? Did you not hear me callin' you?

REGINALD. Oh, I heard you loud and clear. But I knew you weren't possibly calling *my* name, 'cause you were screaming. Thirty-plus years of love and it still ain't stuck. I'm your husband, not your dog—

BANEATTA. You're also always ten minutes *late* to your own service. Punctuality is Godly—

REGINALD. Yeah, yeah, yeah—spare me your sermon and help me with this here tie.

> *Baneatta assists Reginald with his tie. She about chokes him as she ties it.*

I couldn't sleep last night, honey. I kept tossin' and turnin'—

BANEATTA. I know, I was there.

REGINALD. I think I'ma little nervous. I—…I have to make your father proud. This is my first sermon as their new pastor, and Bernard left me some mighty big shoes to fill. I ain't just stepping into his robe, I'm stepping into his legacy. His eulogy has to be perfect.

BANEATTA. And it will be—

REGINALD. But what if—

BANEATTA. Aun-aun-aun. *Reggie.* "We walk by faith and not by—"

REGINALD and BANEATTA. "Sight."

> *Baneatta kisses him on the cheek.*

REGINALD. Thank you, honey. *(Beat.)* And how you holdin' up? Them eyes look kinda sad to me—

BANEATTA. *(Lying with attitude.)* I'm *fine*, thank you very much—

REGINALD. You didn't sound fine screamin' into that phone—

BANEATTA. Can we go?

REGINALD. Wait, Baneatta. Hey-hey-hey, slow down now. You be honest with me. I know how tough today is, but I don't want you hiding your grief. We can talk about it—

BANEATTA. God and I have already talked it out—

REGINALD. But, your *husband* can tell somethin' ain't right—

BANEATTA. Nothing's wrong—

REGINALD. Is it your sister? She land safely?

BANEATTA. We always ten minutes late—

REGINALD. Don't avoid me, now—

BANEATTA. *(Slightly exploding.)* I DUNNO! Beverly only calls me when she needs money, and burying Daddy required spending money, which Beverly has *none* of. So, who knows where she is—

REGINALD. *(Beat.)* That little talk with Jesus didn't go very well, did it?

BANEATTA. *(Putting out her hand.)* The car keys?—

REGINALD. Are staying in my pocket until my wife takes a deep breath with me. Come here, woman…

Poutingly, Baneatta obeys. She walks over to him.

BANEATTA. I—

REGINALD. Aye, Aye, Aye, now. Hush. Burying a parent is never easy. *(Beat.)* So, let yourself feel whatever you need to feel today. Don't go being strong for everybody else. Baneatta, let *me* be strong for *you*. That's why I'm here. Now, let's start this day off with some peace and calm. Just like your father said: "One big deep breath now."

Reginald inhales for a deep breath as Baneatta exhales the shortest possible breath.

Alright, ugh, let's try that again.

They try again. This time Baneatta breathes deeply with him.

Theeeeeere we go, beautiful! Aha! There's that smile I fell in love with—

BANEATTA. Oh, stop it—

REGINALD. Honey, your smile turns my light on *every time*—

BANEATTA. Don't you start nothin' you can't finish—

REGINALD. I always do—

BANEATTA. *(Jokingly.)* Barely! Can we go now?

REGINALD. Yes, we can. But, promise me you'll lean on me today. I'm right here for my woman.

BANEATTA. Thank you, and you look at me from that pulpit if you need me.

REGINALD. I will. Ooh, I love you, sweet thang.

BANEATTA. I love you too, sugar bear. Now come on, I bet Beverly done beat us to the chapel.

>*As Reginald and Baneatta exit, lights shift to Beverly Jenkins, who's smoking a cigarette while having quite the time shifting her breasts into place. Her daughter, La'Trice, sits in a corner chair, eyes glued to her phone.*

LA'TRICE. Ma, I don't think we spose to smoke in this hotel room—

BEVERLY. La'Trice, I don't think you're paying for us to *stay* in this hotel room, so mind ya business—

LA'TRICE. I'm just saying—

BEVERLY. Say less. And put that *damn* phone down. You need to read a book.

LA'TRICE. I *am* reading—

BEVERLY. What?

LA'TRICE. …Facebook.

>*La'Trice giggles to herself.*

BEVERLY. I should slap you. *(Beat.)* Okay, anyway…tell me baby. How do the puppies look?

>*Beverly swivels around, revealing her well-oiled breasts. La'Trice looks up from her phone in shock.*

LA'TRICE. Are you wearing that in public?

BEVERLY. Are you questioning my fashion? What's the problem?

LA'TRICE. It's not a problem, but your breasts got more oil than your elbows. Ain't we going to church?

BEVERLY. It's holy oil!

LA'TRICE. *(Beat.)* I guess… Well, you definitely showin' the congregation *everything* God blessed you with—

BEVERLY. AND MORE! They say the best place to find a husband is inside *God's* house, and that's *exactly* what Beverly will be doing. 'Cause your triflin' daddy ain't good for nothin' but that child support check. So, every *new* day is an opportuni*tay*.

LATRICE. Even at Grandpa's funeral?

BEVERLY. *(Dramatically snapping.)* It *ain't* a funeral, it's a celebration! That's the problem with Black folk, our mindset. Always stuck in tradition. Why we gotta wear black, huh? We *already* Black! We should be honoring my daddy in style, *COLOR*! Hell, canary yellow was his favorite, and he wore it like a *pimp*. Shit, he taught me good fashion!

LA'TRICE. *(Beat.)* Did he?

BEVERLY. Shut up…

> *Now insecure from La'Trice's comments, Beverly slightly covers herself.*

And go put your shoes on. I called the Uber five minutes ago. If your Aunt Baneatta beats us to that church, I'll never hear the end of it.

LA'TRICE. *(Beat.)* Ma?

BEVERLY. Yeah, baby?

LA'TRICE. Do I gotta watch them put Grandpa B in the ground?

BEVERLY. Whatcha mean?

LA'TRICE. When we buried Grandma Rita, they covered her casket with dirt and lowered her into the ground. I can still see it in my head. I don't want a casket to be the last time I see B.

BEVERLY. Me neither. *(Beat.)* We can leave before that part.

LA'TRICE. Thank you, Ma. *(Beat.)* I'm sorry he's gone.

> *La'Trice notices Beverly is having a moment. She hugs her in the silence. Just as La'Trice lets go:*

BEVERLY. But La'Trice, I hope you know that ain't the last time you gon' see him, right? When they lower our bodies into the dirt, we believe our *spirits* rise on up to heaven. So this ain't goodbye, baby. It's see you later. *(Beat.)* I think your Grandma Rita is the happiest she's been in a long time—

LA'TRICE. Why?!

BEVERLY. 'Cause your Grandpa B just pimp-walked his ass through them pearly gates. Ohh, I know her face lit up when she saw him. I bet they're having the sweetest slow-dancin' reunion in heaven right now. Just cuttin' a rug, like they used to. You think about that?

LA'TRICE. No, I guess I didn't.

BEVERLY. Well, don't forget that part, honey, that's the best part.

LA'TRICE. You right, Mama—

BEVERLY. I know I'm right! That's why today is a celebration! *That's* why the puppies are out!

Beverly begins a boob dance.

Joy, joy, joy, joy, joy, joy, joy. No sadness up in here today, baby girl. This is Daddy's party, his finale! We sendin' him out with a bang. Bam!

LA'TRICE. Bam! I'm down!

They share a quick two-step.

BEVERLY. But wait! Before we leave, La'Trice, you gotta promise me somethin'—

LA'TRICE. Yeah, Mama?

BEVERLY. You stay right by my side and keep ya ass quiet, ya hear?

LA'TRICE. Yes, Mama—

BEVERLY. No, I'm serious! You like to get cute in front of company and run ya damn mouth too much. Keep it shut. You know how crazy our family is and I don't wanna have to slap nobody on today. Your mama's workin' on being a better *Christian. (Beat.)* So, don't pull no shit—

LA'TRICE. Okay, okay. I got it, dang!

BEVERLY. *(Playfully.)* You better! *(Beat.)* We ain't seen some of these folks since the last funeral. I think your favorite cousin Kenny's coming—

LA'TRICE. HE IS! Ooh, I can't wait to see him.

BEVERLY. Me too, it's been way too long. Shoot, the Uber's here girl. Put ya shoes on, let's go!

La'Trice exits as Beverly takes one final glance in the mirror.
One big deep breath now.
> *With her breath, the lights fade as other lights rise on Kenny and Logan. They stand at the New Haven train station with duffle bags in hand.*

LOGAN. *(So anxious.)* Are you sure this is a good idea?

KENNY. Logan—

LOGAN. I feel like *you* think it's good, but my chakra is sending an amber alert.

KENNY. Our Lyft is three minutes away—

LOGAN. I'm a Jew—

KENNY. I'm aware—

LOGAN. A Jew who's never step foot inside a synagogue, let alone a Black church.

KENNY. You'll survive—

LOGAN. I'm penetrating a private cultural tradition—

KENNY. Why penetrating?—

LOGAN. It's like a reverse *Get Out* and we all know how that ended. *(Beat.)* I should've stayed home and sent my condolences in a nice Hallmark card or a Bundt cake. That's what huh-white people do well—

KENNY. Ohh-kay…relax. You'll be fine. Our funerals are more like family reunions. By the end of the night, it's a full-on party.

LOGAN. You're making shit up, funerals are never parties—

KENNY. Black funerals are. The fainting, the wigs, the pinky toes hanging on for dear life. Ooooh and that one soloist who always grabs the mic, but doesn't know a *single* lyric. Just you wait! After today, you'll be begging for a season pass—

LOGAN. Not if your mother's there.

KENNY. Here we go—

LOGAN. You-know-she-hates-me!

KENNY. Today is not about my mother, it's about B. The *only* grandparent to accept me as the faggot that I am. He loved you because he loved me, and I know he'd want you at his funeral.

LOGAN. But your *mother* is at his funeral—

KENNY. *(Irritated.)* Babe—

LOGAN. Babe, every time she sees me, it's like I'm not in the room. I get grilled from head to toe, then she just walks on past. It's like when Casey Nicholaw cut me from that *Mormon* callback—

KENNY. You said you were over that—

LOGAN. I AM! But if I don't speak, she won't. So, I have to initiate: "Hi Baneatta," I say, every time, as butch as humanly possible. But what do I get back? Thanks for asking, NOTHING! ABSOLUTELY NOTHING, but a timid dog paw, followed by her legendary eye squint, concluding in an Oscar award–winning, wait for it… *(Beat.)* "Yes." Every time, like clockwork—And my name? Oy vey! She's called me everything in the book but Logan. Lavender. Lentil! Lamar? I swear one time she said Loofah!

KENNY. Yeah, she definitely said Loofah.

LOGAN. See! She ignores the fact that we've been together *four* years, and it stings. Plus, when *you* get around her, you—

Logan stops himself.

KENNY. *(Beat.)* I…I—what?

LOGAN. Nevermind—

KENNY. Oh no, no, no, Kellyanne! We're live, keep going.

Logan doesn't respond.

Heller?

Logan takes a deep breath.

LOGAN. *(Reluctantly.)* You say you're proud to love me, but the moment we get around your mother, you run back in the closet—

KENNY. I do not—

LOGAN. Actually, you do. Your whole demeanor changes. It's like watching a little boy be punished for stealing candy, and I'm the little boy. I stole her son from her.

KENNY. No, you didn't—

LOGAN. *(Firm at first.)* You can't see it from the outside, so you don't really know, do you?

KENNY. I *know*, I want the love of my life by my side when I face my family. Please don't let my mother ruin that for me.

> *The Lyft arrives. Kenny slides in, leaving Logan on the sidewalk.*

(To driver.) For Kenny, yeah? *(Beat.)* Thanks. *(Beat.)* Yep, St. Luke's. Not too far.

> *After a breath, Logan joins him.*

LOGAN. Okay. *(Beat.)* I'll stand with you.

KENNY. Thank you.

LOGAN. I just hope I don't die.

> *Kenny snaps Logan a look.*

I'm done.

KENNY. You remember that first time you met B?

LOGAN. *(Beat.)* Like it was yesterday.

KENNY. You were just as nervous then as you are right now. I swear you peed yourself—

LOGAN. Kellyanne has no comment.

KENNY. Yeah, he looked you dead in the eye and said: "Boy, you break my grandson's heart and I'll snap your little white ass in half."

LOGAN. That's when I peed.

KENNY. But, that meant he liked you. *(Beat.)* I never told you this but, later that night, he pulled me in the kitchen and whispered: "Ken-Ken, if that Logan boy makes you happy, he's alright by me. I want you happy. You keep him close. Don't you let him go, for *nobody*." I can still hear that voice.

> *Kenny has a moment.*

So you're staying close to me today. We are waltzing our *gay asses* in that church, and if anybody gives heat, I'll deal with them.

LOGAN. Okay.

KENNY. *(To driver.)* Thanks, this is good here.

The two exit the car. Kenny spots Beverly adjusting "the puppies" from afar.

OH DEAR GOD, it begins.

LOGAN. Wha—?! Oh shit, is that her nipple? Who is that?—

KENNY. My crazy Aunt Bev.

LOGAN. The hairdresser from Atlanta?

KENNY. Bingo!

LOGAN. I see. Well, she *sorta* looks fierce.

KENNY. Exactly…

KENNY and LOGAN. *(Cocking their heads sideways.)* Sorta.

Laughter is shared.

KENNY. Hey. We got this, baby. I love you, kisses.

Kenny perks out his lips. They kiss.

LOGAN. I love you too.

Lights dim on Kenny and Logan while rising on Beverly and La'Trice, who walk onto the church steps.

LA'TRICE. Oooh MAMA, WAIT! I think that's Kenny.

BEVERLY. Alright, we'll see him inside—

LA'TRICE. But who is that white boy with 'em?

BEVERLY. No-no-no, see! You already mindin' other folks' business. Cut it!

Simone walks in.

SIMONE. Aunt Bev, is that you?

BEVERLY. There's only one!… And look at my favorite niece.

SIMONE. I'm your only niece.

BEVERLY. *(Beat.)* Girl, shut up and hug me.

Beverly and Simone hug.

Ooohf, you been eatin'? You feelin' mighty skinty! You on that Jenny Craig, ain't you? It's too expensive for me—

SIMONE. No Aunty, I'm the same size I've always been.

BEVERLY. Well praise God for maintenance!

SIMONE. And you look—

BEVERLY. Cinched... I know! Cardio keeps these thighs tight, but I made sure not to lose my trunk, okay? Squats, BAM! She's still sitting! La'Trice, get over here and say hi to your cousin. You remember Simone, don't you?

LA'TRICE. *(Dry.)* No—

BEVERLY. Yes, you do! Though I guess y'all ain't seen each other since we buried Mommy. That was a decade ago—

SIMONE. How you doing, little cuz? You look cute.

LA'TRICE. I know.

BEVERLY. La'Trice! *(To Simone.)* Your parents ain't here yet, are they?

SIMONE. I dunno, I just arrived.

BEVERLY. Well, I hope we beat 'em. Wait! You ain't here by yaself, are you? Where's that big-footed stack of chocolate mus-cul who proposed to you?—

SIMONE. *(Stone cold.)* He called off our engagement and is now dating the white woman he cheated on me with—

LA'TRICE. Oh, *HELL* no—

Beverly checks La'Trice with a daring glare.

SIMONE. It's okay. It's fine—

BEVERLY. No, it ain't! I'm sorry darlin', I hadn't heard. *(Beat.)* Well *chile* look, consider it a blessin'. I didn't know how to say this before, but uh...his ass was *ugly* anyway. Teeth all backwards, you can do much better than that—

SIMONE. Everybody says that—

BEVERLY. It's true! Hell, forget him—ya know what?! Tonight, after we bury Daddy, we are goin' to the club—

SIMONE. No, we are not—

BEVERLY. *Yes*, we are!

SIMONE. No, we are not—

BEVERLY. They say the best way to get over an ex, is to get under, the next. *BAM!*

SIMONE. You have lost your mind!—

BEVERLY. But kept my figure.

21

LA'TRICE. Ma, I'm hungry—

BEVERLY. I don't wanna hear it, La'Trice. I told you to grab a snack from that vending machine, but *you* were too busy TikToking. So TikTok your ass on back to that phone and look at pictures of food—

LA'TRICE. That ain't fair!—

BEVERLY. Life ain't fair—

SIMONE. I think I have a granola bar in my purse—

LA'TRICE. I don't eat granola—

SIMONE. Well, you'll starve today.

Baneatta and Reginald arrive.

REGINALD. HEEY, NOW! There's my baby girl.

SIMONE. Daddy, you know I'm grown and Kenny's the baby.

REGINALD. You never too grown to be *my* baby girl. Now, hug ya father.

Reginald and Simone hug.

LA'TRICE. Hiiii, Aunty!

BANEATTA. Hi sweet pea, you look cute.

LA'TRICE. Thank you. I know!

Simone hugs her mother.

SIMONE. Hey Ma, how you holding up?

BANEATTA. Better now that you're here.

Baneatta kisses Simone.

BEVERLY. SIIIIIIS!

Beverly approaches Baneatta, arms wide.

BANEATTA. *(Appalled.)* OOOOOHHH!

Baneatta deflects the hug. Instead, she pulls Beverly in for air kisses, and then:

What in God's name are you wearin'?

BEVERLY. That's not the way to greet your sister—

BANEATTA. Your titties greeted me first—

BEVERLY. Oh please, it's just a little lace to add some flavor—

BANEATTA. It's flavor*less*—

LA'TRICE. Told you, Ma!

BEVERLY. SHUT UP, LA'TRICE! It ain't my fault God blessed me with all this glory—

BANEATTA. Don't you blame *that* on God.

REGINALD. Baneatta, why don't we head inside?

BANEATTA. *REGINALD!*

REGINALD. That's my cue—

Reginald exits.

SIMONE. La'Trice, come with me. Let's try and find you some food.

LA'TRICE. THANK YOU! Jeesh.

BEVERLY. Stay with your cousin and keep your mouth shut. Ya hear?

LA'TRICE. Yes, Ma.

La'Trice and Simone enter the church. The tension lingers between the sisters as they put on airs for arriving guests. Then:

BEVERLY. *(Hurt.)* Why you gotta do that?

BANEATTA. Do what?!

BEVERLY. Embarrass me.

BANEATTA. You embarrassed yourself showing up to Daddy's funeral with your titties tap dancin' out cha top—

BEVERLY. IT'S A PUSH-UP BRA!

BANEATTA. *(Gasped.)* No?!

BEVERLY. I just wanted to start this day off with some sisterly love, but you can't even do that. What does that say?

BANEATTA. It says I don't approve of your titties—

BEVERLY. Well, I'm sorry you don't *approve*, Baneatta. I've never lived up to your expectations no way, so why start today?!

BANEATTA. That ain't true—

BEVERLY. It is! You been nasty and bossy to me, since we were tiny girls. And it took me decades to understand why, but I done figured it out. You're jealous. I'm the younger, *thinner*, and prettier sister—

BANEATTA. Beverly, what do you have for me to be jealous of, huh?

I own a home, you rent a two-bedroom. I'm a tenured professor with a husband and two cars. While you couldn't keep a man if you paid him to stay. I've earned two degrees, while you're a college dropout. All I've tried to do is push you towards the path Mama and Daddy wanted for us—

BEVERLY. WANTED FOR YOU! What they wanted for *you*.

BANEATTA. Look at us, we ain't even in the sanctuary yet and we're bickerin'—

BEVERLY. You started it! *(Beat.)* All I needed was a hug from my big sister, but instead I get your riches thrown in my face. But that don't faze me none *Baneatta*, 'cause I'm happy with the little I got. I make enough money now to give us a good life.

Beverly begins to walk away.

And another thang: I'm a grown *assss* woman, so I'll wear whatever the hell I *want* to my daddy's funeral /

BANEATTA. WATCH YOUR MOUTH on the steps of God's house—

KENNY. Heeey Ma!

Unaware, Kenny and Logan approach. Kenny runs to hug Baneatta. Logan avoids her at all costs.

BANEATTA. *(Switch-hitting.)* Hi, baby—

KENNY. You look good! How you feelin'?

BANEATTA. I was fine 'til a couple minutes ago.

KENNY. What's wrong—

BEVERLY. Your mother, always! I *cannot* believe my eyes, you handsome devil. Get over here and hug your favorite aunty.

Kenny moves to hug her.

KENNY. You're my only aunty. It's good to see you, Aunt Bev—

BEVERLY. It's good to be seen. Now, *who* is this beautiful *huh*-white man next to you?

KENNY. Ma, you remember Lo/

BANEATTA. *LUCAS*, yes, your little *friend*...Lucas. Who you failed to mention would be joining us when we spoke on the phone.

KENNY. I didn't know I had to—

24

BEVERLY. Oh, hi *Lucas*—

LOGAN. It's actually—

BEVERLY. Such a pleasure to meet you! I'm Beverly, the fiercest aunt to walk the runway.

LOGAN. Nice to meet you, Beverly.

BANEATTA. Kenneth, we'll discuss this in private. I should check in with the funeral director—

As Baneatta leaves:

LOGAN. It's good to see you, Baneatta.

Time clicks into slow motion. Baneatta tuns back, barely reaching her wrist out like a dog paw. Her eyes tighten as she looks through Logan's soul.

BANEATTA. *(Beat.)* Yes. Beverly, *please* adjust yourself. I'll see you two inside.

Baneatta exits into the church.

LOGAN. Welp, add Lucas to the list!

BEVERLY. Don't let her faze you, *Lucas*, she hates anything breathing—

KENNY. You're talking about my mother—

BEVERLY. She was my sister before she was your mother. The truth hurts, okay?—

KENNY. Aunty, his name is *Logan*, not Lucas.

BEVERLY. Oh, I'm sorry darlin'. I thought she said Lucas—

LOGAN and KENNY. *She did*—

KENNY. Don't let it get to you, it's a tough day for her—

BEVERLY. It's a tough day for *all* of us. Baneatta ain't the only one with feelings!

KENNY. Aunty, can we not do this right now? Let's get inside.

Kenny moves towards the entrance.

BEVERLY. STOP! Wait! Hold. *(Beat.)* Y'all *gays* know good fashion. Tell Aunty the truth. How do I look?

Beverly twirls on herself. The two stare, dumbstruck.

Well…somebody say something!

LOGAN. Um…okay… What exactly, are you going…for?

BEVERLY. Uhh…Wakanda…marriageable…not too thotty-otty now, but flexible!

LOGAN and KENNY. *(Beat.)* YASSSSS!

BEVERLY. YASSS!

LOGAN. There's definitely a version of that in there…somewhere—

BEVERLY. Aunty still got it, right?

LOGAN. Yes…   KENNY. Uh-huh…

BEVERLY. BAM!

LOGAN. BAM! Oooh, wow. I told Kenny you look fierce.

> *Beverly grabs Logan's arm and proceeds inside.*

BEVERLY. Ooh Kenny, I like him already.

> *Kenny follows suit. Inside, Baneatta is discovered with a vibrating cell phone in her hand. She ferociously presses end. Reginald appears.*

REGINALD. *(Calling.)* BANEATTA!

BANEATTA. *(Sternly.)* Yes, Reginald.

REGINALD. You and your sister talk it out?

BANEATTA. I don't have a sister—

REGINALD. Baneatta—

BANEATTA. Her titties are doing the tango outta her blouse—

REGINALD. Don't let that distract you from your daddy—

BANEATTA. And your dern son done brought that boy with him: *Lorenzo.*

REGINALD. *Baneatta—*

BANEATTA. It's sin and he knows it.

REGINALD. Slow down—

BANEATTA. Embarrassing me on a day like this. Daddy's probably rollin' around in his grave—

REGINALD. Listen here, now—

BANEATTA. NOBODY HAS ANY REVERENCE OR DECENCY

LEFT! Folks just do *what* they want and expect God to bless 'em anyway. It don't work like that!

REGINALD. Alright!

Reginald walks away.

BANEATTA. Reggie, where you going?

REGINALD. Before we left, you promised you'd lean on me. But, here you are twisting yourself into a tizzy. If you won't let me speak, why am I standing here, huh? Is somethin' else going on, Baneatta? 'Cause this ain't like you. I need you today *too*, remember? *(Beat.)* Now, I'ma go focus on your father's eulogy. Today should be a day of memories and healing for the family, not chaos. You find me when you've calm down.

Reginald exits.

BANEATTA. *(Calling to him.)* Reggie!

Baneatta's phone buzzes again as the lights shift to Simone and La'Trice in the church kitchen. Simone hands La'Trice bread.

LA'TRICE. This is white, I only eat wheat—

SIMONE. Be lucky I found you something—

LA'TRICE. They ain't got no jelly or nothin'? Useless!

SIMONE. You sound mighty ungrateful for someone who don't pay her own bills.

LA'TRICE. *(Sucking her teeth.) Ill*, now you sound like my mama. I have gratitude!

SIMONE. You do?! Did you leave it in Atlanta? 'Cause I've witnessed far more attitude than gratitude, La'Trice. When I was fifteen, being fed was enough—

LA'TRICE. *Sixteen!* I'll be *sixteen* in three weeks, so let's round up. Ocklurrr? *(Beat.)* What you buyin' me?

SIMONE. *(Beat.)* Nothin'! You don't remember meeting me, but suddenly you want birthday gifts? The Devil is a lie!—

LA'TRICE. You remember meetin' me?

Simone is cornered with the truth.

Got 'em! A Amazon gift card is perfect. Fifty dollahs.

SIMONE. To buy what?!

LA'TRICE. I dunno yet, that's why it's a *gift card*.

SIMONE. You are definitely your mother's child.

LA'TRICE. What's that supposed to mean?

SIMONE. It'll make sense in due time, now hurry up.

La'Trice offers bread.

LA'TRICE. You want some?

SIMONE. No, I'm good. But we need to get back.

LA'TRICE. *(Biting into the bread.)* I don't wanna go back. Not if Ma and Aunty gon' be fightin' like that the whole time. Simone, why they hate each other? Like, ain't we suppose to be family?

SIMONE. "Family," is a loaded word—

LA'TRICE. I see.

SIMONE. And I wouldn't say they *hate* each other, per se, but they definitely see the world through different sunglasses.

LA'TRICE. *(Trying to up Simone.)* And *lenses*.

SIMONE. But, somewhere deep down, I think they really just want what's best for the other. That's why they argue. It's a sister thing.

LA'TRICE. Huh, a sister thing. I wanted a sister.

SIMONE. What happened?

LA'TRICE. I realized she'd be dipping in my Christmas presents and who needs that?

SIMONE. Aha—

LA'TRICE. And a father. *(Beat.)* I mean like, I *have* a father, but he ain't raising me. Ma and him don't vibe, so he's just a check. But a check ain't a father. Like, keep your check, I want your time. Sometimes I wonder, like, who would I be if he was here. But he ain't. *(Beat.)* Sorry, my bad. How did I get there—

SIMONE. No sorrys, we can talk about it—

LA'TRICE. Nah-nah, let's talk about *you*. You ever want a sister?

SIMONE. Umm…no. I was the princess of the house for three years 'til nappy-headed Kenny popped outta nowhere and stole *all* my Christmas presents—

LA'TRICE. Point, proven—

SIMONE. And, ooooh, did they spoil him! Daddy finally got the boy he prayed for and it felt like he just forgot about me—

LA'TRICE. Like my daddy—

SIMONE. Wait-wait-wait, hold on now. Let's talk this out. *(Beat.)* Your father is still alive, right?

LA'TRICE. Yeah, but dead to us.

SIMONE. It doesn't sound like he's dead to *you*. It sounds to me like you got a lot of questions and I think they all deserve answers. So, Ms. "Soon-to-be-sixteen," can I drop some wisdom on you?

LA'TRICE. Maybe.

SIMONE. Don't assume he's forgotten about you. That's not fair. You wanna relationship with your own father, go build one. They may not get along, but that doesn't mean y'all can't. You put that phone you're always on to good use, and call him. Miscommunication ruins a lot of love. *(Beat.)* Can you promise me you'll try calling?

LA'TRICE. *(Beat.)* Yeah...I guess I could do dat. *(Beat.)* But can you promise *me* somethin'?

SIMONE. What?

LA'TRICE. That gift card!

SIMONE. Oh my Lord, what am I gonna do with you?

LA'TRICE. Be the sister I never had.

SIMONE. You know that means we gon' argue.

LA'TRICE. I'm ready!

Laughter is shared.

SIMONE. Deal.

La'Trice surprises Simone with a hug.

LA'TRICE. You mad cool, Simone. Why ya man leave you for a Becky?—

SIMONE. *(Avoiding.)* OKAAY! I think it's time to get you back to your mother—

LA'TRICE. Don't dodge my question—

SIMONE. We'll talk about these raggedy men when you're old enough—

LA'TRICE. I know about 'em—

SIMONE. You betta not. Come on, let's go!

>   *Simone leads La'Trice out of the kitchen. We pick up on Kenny, Beverly, and Logan entering the church lobby. Beverly is still arm-locked with Logan.*

BEVERLY. Woof, Logan!… These mus-culs, I'm flashin'—

KENNY. Where is everybody?

BEVERLY. Probably hidin' from your mama—

KENNY. Enough, Aunty—

>   *Kenny peers into the chapel windows.*

Well, the congregation is settled and the choir is singing, but Daddy ain't in the pulpit yet. They must be waiting on us.

BEVERLY. Lord, I pray they done captured my daddy's more handsomer features. Sometimes you go to these funerals and the body's *all* jacked up. Eyebrows extra arched, face makeup don't match the neck. One eye opened—one eye closed, just a mess—

LOGAN. I'm sure he looks lovely—

BEVERLY. And I *hate* these flowers. Ya mama didn't ask my opinion—

KENNY. Aunt Bev, please be positive—

BEVERLY. The truth is positive!

>   *Baneatta enters.*

KENNY. There she is! Ma, we 'bout ready to go in?

BANEATTA. Yes, as soon as everybody *covers up*.

BEVERLY. Help me, Jesus. Help me!

>   *Simone and La'Trice enter.*

LA'TRICE. *(Shouting.)* OH MY GOD, Cousin Kenny!

>   *La'Trice runs to hug Kenny.*

KENNY. La'Trice! Wow, look-at-you girl. Somebody got big—

LA'TRICE. *(Slightly offended.)* What you tryin' to say?

KENNY. Big, as in tall. You had a growth spurt since Grandma's funeral.

LA'TRICE. You right! Mama says I get my height from my daddy—
BEVERLY. That's *all* you got from your daddy—
KENNY. Well, I like it.
LA'TRICE. Thank you, Kenny. I been waitin' to see you. I got a verse or two for your ears later.
KENNY. Okay, they ready!
LA'TRICE. Ma, who dis white boy on your arm?
BANEATTA. Good question—
BEVERLY. La'Trice!—
KENNY. His name isn't "white boy" it's Logan and he's my—

Baneatta clears her throat. Kenny and Baneatta catch eyes. Kenny becomes that kid in the candy store.

Friend.
LOGAN. Friend?!
SIMONE. Oh, *that* friend?
KENNY. And hello to you too, sis.

Kenny and Simone hug.

SIMONE. Hey, little bro.
KENNY. You been eating? You lookin' kinda snatched—
BEVERLY. Jenny Craig! I said it—
SIMONE. *(Annoyed.) YES*, I'm eating. No one seems to notice anything about *me* in this family 'til somebody else dies.
KENNY. Okay, relax. It was just an observation.
SIMONE. Speaking of—

Simone clears her throat, shifting her focus to Logan.

Hiii, *Larry*…we've never officially met, but I've heard such great things through my mother.
KENNY. Like what?
SIMONE. I'm Simone, the older sister. And what do you do, Larry?
LOGAN. Logan—
SIMONE. Sure.

Simone offers the same dog paw as Baneatta.

LOGAN. I'm an actor, too. We met on a contract.

BEVERLY. *(To Simone.)* Ain't he cute, girl?

SIMONE. If you're into that.

LA'TRICE. Into what?

BEVERLY. Mind yo business! Get over here.

> *Reginald enters dressed in his pastoral robe, Bible in hand.*

REGINALD. Oh good, everybody's here. We need to hurry up. Mother Jones has been remixing "Amazing Grace" on loop for the past half hour, and it *ain't* so amazin'. There's my son.

KENNY. Hey, Dad!!

> *Kenny and Reginald hug.*

REGINALD. Whoo-boy, you clean up well! I wonder who taught you?!

KENNY. You!   REGINALD. Me!

> *They share a laugh.*

You remember Logan?

REGINALD. *(Shaking Logan's hand.)* I sure do. Good to see you again, son. Thanks for being here.

LOGAN. My pleasure.

REGINALD. Alright, everybody. Let's circle up for family prayer.

LA'TRICE. Is this white boy in the family?

BEVERLY. La'Trice, shut-it-up!—

BANEATTA. No, she's right. This is the *family* processional—

LOGAN. I-I can go sit inside. I don't want to disturb you—

REGINALD. Son, you're fine right where you are—

BEVERLY. I'd say so—

BANEATTA. Nobody asked you—

REGINALD. EVERYONE, bow your heads and *please* shut your mouths.

> *They all grab hands and circle up. Logan is awkwardly stuck between Baneatta and Kenny.*

Heavenly Father, please forgive us, for I think we've all forgotten *why* we're here. We're *here*, to celebrate the life and legacy of our beloved Bernard Jenkins—

BEVERLY. *(Overacted.)* YES, LORT! Thank you Lort—

    Baneatta sucks her teeth.

REGINALD. Bernard was a pillar of laughter and *kindness*. And I know he'd want us *lovin'* on one another right now instead of bickering over the small things.

BEVERLY. YES, GOD! Let the small things go. Go-go-go-go-go—

LA'TRICE. *(Embarrassed.)* Ma, hush—

    Beverly squeezes La'Trice's hand.

Ouch—

BANEATTA. Shhhh.

    Baneatta's cell phone begins to buzz again. She breaks the prayer circle to silence it, but can't quite figure out how.

REGINALD. SO, we thank You oh bless-ed Father for giving us yet another opportunity to come together as a family, *new* members included.

BEVERLY. *(Whispering.)* I told you to turn that phone off—

LA'TRICE. I did, that ain't mine.

REGINALD. Give us Your strength, oh Lord, as we head inside to view Bernard's body. For though he is now absent from this bitter earth, we know his spirit *forever* lives in You.

BANEATTA, BEVERLY, SIMONE, and KENNY. *(Ad-libs.)* Yes Lord. / That's right. / Yes he does. / Oh yes.

REGINALD. Thank you for all these things. In Your precious name, amen.

ALL. Amen.

    Reginald approaches Baneatta just as she silences the phone.

REGINALD. Was that your phone again? Who keeps callin' you?

BANEATTA. Uh…it was an alarm, but it's off now. Reggie, I'm sorry 'bout earlier. I got a little caught up. But you're right, I need to focus. Today is Daddy's day.

REGINALD. That's right, just focus on Bernard, and let that Logan boy be. He ain't botherin' nobody.

Lights shift to Logan and Kenny.

LOGAN. I'm ordering a Lyft—

KENNY. Why? Where you go—

LOGAN. Your "*friend,*" Lucas, can still make the twelve thirty back to the city—

KENNY. Logan—

LOGAN. "I got you baby, if anyone gives heat, I'll deal with them." Liar.

KENNY. I'm sorry—

LOGAN. You promised. You promised me you wouldn't cower and that's exactly what you did.

KENNY. I got flustered. My mother—

LOGAN. Does-not-want-me here, and neither does your sister—

KENNY. Let me /

LOGAN. I want to be here for you, Kenny, but I won't be a punching bag.

KENNY. I know, let's just get through the service—

LOGAN. NO ONE WANTS ME AT THE SERVICE—

Lights shift to La'Trice and Beverly.

LA'TRICE. Ooooh Ma, white boy is screaming at Kenny. I'm down to *bop* if we need to!—

BEVERLY. You ain't bopping nobody, and stop callin' him "white boy." He has a name. It's *Lucas*! If I can remember it, so-can-you.

KENNY. Logan, please don't embarrass me in front of my entire family.

LOGAN. I'm already your embarrassment.

Simone approaches.

SIMONE. Helloooo, Thespians. Y'all *straight* over here?

KENNY. YES, Simone, we're great.

SIMONE. Didn't sound like it—

REGINALD. *(Clapping his hands.)* Alright now, the ushers are opening the church doors. Take as much time as you need at the casket. He looks peaceful.

Reginald grabs Baneatta's hand.

You ready?

BANEATTA. As ready as I'll ever be.

The church doors swing open. A shimmering maroon casket appears onstage. There's a loud organ playing an interesting version of "Amazing Grace."

Reginald and Baneatta lead the way, arms locked. Simone is behind the two of them. La'Trice and Beverly follow after Simone. Kenny puts out his hand and, after much hesitation, Logan falls in line at the tail end with him.

Everyone has a moment over Bernard's casket. Baneatta is the first. She takes a long moment to stare at Bernard in silence. And then:

Look at 'em. He looks good, *real* good. My sweet daddy done gone on home.

Baneatta begins to break down. Reginald consoles her. He pulls her away and sits her in the pew. Simone steps in to get her look at Bernard.

SIMONE. You still grinning, B, just like you always did. But, that right side is a little higher than the left. Uh-oh. *(Beat.)* Your peach is gonna make you proud, ya hear me?

Simone walks to the pew. She hugs Baneatta. La'Trice and Beverly hold hands at the casket. Beverly doesn't speak, she rocks back and forth, dramatically moaning.

LA'TRICE. Ma, you alright? *(Long beat.)* You gon' make it?

BEVERLY. *(Slowly unraveling.)* Oooh, they done put him in that canary yellow tie I bought him two Christmases back. I ain't seen it on 'em 'til now. *(Growing with dramatic intensity.)* OOOH LAWD, MY DADDY GONE!

BANEATTA. Here come the fireworks!

Beverly begins to fall out.

BEVERLY. HE GONE WITH THE WIND AND HE AIN'T COMIN' BACK—

LA'TRICE. MA, HOLD YOUR WEIGHT, you know you heavy—

BEVERLY. JESUS, JESUS, JESUS, WHY YOU TAKE HIM FROM ME?!—

BANEATTA. He should've taken her—

BEVERLY. Help me Lort! HELP ME!

> *Beverly almost completely falls out. La'Trice catches Beverly and walks her to the pew. Kenny steps forward over Bernard, Logan gives him space.*

KENNY. You saw me like no one else does in this family. What am I gonna do without you?

> *Kenny turns from the casket and the two file into the family pew. A god awful voiceover of Mother Jones gets progressively louder. It's terrible.*

MOTHER JONES. *(Voiceover.)*
I ONCE, WAS LOST
BUT NOW, I'M FOUND
STILL BLIND, BUT NOW I SEE

LA'TRICE. *(Whispering to Beverly.)* Those ain't the right words, Ma—

BEVERLY. Hush!

> *Reginald quickly rises to the pulpit, defusing the madness. Breaking the fourth wall, he uses the audience as his congregation.*

REGINALD. Alright, alright! That's enough Mother Jones, you sound…*alright*. *(Beat.)* What a blessing it is to gather in the house of the Lord, one more time. Amen?

ALL. *(Ad-libs.)* Amen. / Yes Lord. / That's right.

REGINALD. *(Revving up.)* Did y'all feel that sunshine as the family walked in? Even on days like today, when our hearts are heavy, God sends us little reminders that we are *NOT ALONE*!!

ALL. *(Ad-libs.)* Never alone. / Yes he does. / Alright now.

LOGAN. *(Whispered.)* Why is everyone screaming at him?

KENNY. It's normal, you can too.

LOGAN. I'll pass—

REGINALD. Out of respect for the family's wishes, we are keepin' Bernard's service short and sweet. We've already had our hymn... interpreted. So, now we'll have the family remarks, amen?

ALL. Amen.

REGINALD. Y'all come on up here and share a favorite Bernard memory, whatever's on your heart. But, please keep it to a sweet maximum of three minutes or less—

LOGAN. AMEN!—

KENNY. *(Whispered.)* Not now.

LOGAN. Oh-no.

REGINALD. Or we'll all be here 'til tomorrow night, and "Ain't nobody got time...for *that*!"

> *Reginald revels in his corniness as the congregation barely responds.*

Don't be shy now, or I'll keep ramblin' and nobody wants that.

BEVERLY. No, we don't—

> *Simone slowly rises from her seat.*

REGINALD. Ahh, we got one! And of course, it's my *baby* girl.

SIMONE. Daddy...

REGINALD. I'll hush.

> *Reginald takes his seat as Simone takes the mic.*

SIMONE. Hello everyone. I uh... I'm not usually one to talk much...

KENNY. *(Aside.)* Lies—

SIMONE. But I can't put B in the ground without saying a few words about him. He uh, always made you laugh, whether you wanted to or not. I was kind of a wallflower growing up, so I mostly kept to myself; but that didn't work around B. He'd pull me right outta my shell with his charm. And lookin' back on it now, I'm glad he did. My favorite memories of our quality time, was watching him try to cook. Key word: *try*. Lord, B was a wonderful granddaddy, but a *horrible* chef—

BANEATTA. AMEN!

SIMONE. His "famous chicken and biscuits" was only *famous*, to him.

BEVERLY. Dry, the biscuits were dry.

SIMONE. And he knew it was nasty, 'cause he wouldn't eat it himself. He had no shame, but we were fed. *(Beat.)* One time, B got me good. A little white lie, but since I worshipped the ground he walked on, I took him for his word. When we'd stay at his house for the summer, he'd always sit me on his lap, and bounce me around like popcorn 'til I fell off. Then we'd dance, for as long as his feet could take it. I was Cinderella and he was Prince Charming.

And B always played the same song on repeat, Stevie Wonder's "Isn't She Lovely." So, this *one* day, while we were dancing, he bent down and whispered in my ear: "Peach, you know I'm best friends with Stevie Wonder and he wrote this about you when I told him my first grand had arrived!" Y'all, nappy-headed eight-year-old Simone told everybody at school, from the teachers, to the woman serving mash potatoes in the cafeteria. I sure did. I was *so* proud, and so stupid. *(Beat.)* But as foolish as I was, B made me feel like the only diamond in the world, and I shined. *(Beat.)* To this day, every time I hear "Isn't She Lovely" on the radio, I'm Cinderella all over again. Elegant.

B, *you* were the lovely one. Now, go rest them feet. I know we'll dance again.

> *The congregation applauds as Simone exits the podium. Reginald rises to the pulpit.*

REGINALD. Of course, my baby girl brought us all to tears, how beautiful. Alright now, who's next?

BEVERLY. ME! I got *lots* to say about *my* daddy.

BANEATTA. Lord, hold my mule—

> *Beverly grabs La'Trice's hand.*

LA'TRICE. Ma, I don't wanna get up in front of all these people.

BEVERLY. But you wanna be a rapper?! Oh, you comin' wit me. I might need you to catch me again—

> *Beverly and La'Trice approach the microphone.*

REGINALD. Church, let us welcome Bernard's youngest, Beverly. She's gonna say *a few* words.

> *The congregation applauds.*

BEVERLY. *(Enjoying her moment.)* Thank you, thank you…so much.

BANEATTA. She 'bout to say somethin' *real* stupid, with them *titties* still poppin' out.

SIMONE. Let's hope not.

Beverly and La'Trice are at the mic.

BEVERLY. *Heeeelllllllo.* Is this thing on?

Beverly taps the microphone, it echos.

Oh shit—shoot. Sorry, that was, my bad. Umm, thank y'all for comin' out to celebrate *my* daddy. As Reggie said, I am Bernard's *youngest*. The baby. The cutest. The promise. *(Beat.)* And this here is *my* baby girl, La'Trice Franklin. I gave her her daddy's last name, though we ain't seen him in a while. Pray for us. La'Trice, come up here and say hi to the church folk—

Terrified, La'Trice approaches the mic.

LA'TRICE. Umm, what's good, fam? My new mixtape, *Homie's Paradise,* is dropping on Tidal this winter—

BEVERLY. Okay, back it up. That's enough!

Beverly points La'Trice back to her seat.

BANEATTA. Just embarrassing—

KENNY. This is too good—

BEVERLY. Uh, it ain't easy burying Daddy today. This feels harder than when Mama left us… *(Beat.)* Growing up, I just knew my parents were invincible. They showered us with so much love, it fooled me into believin' they'd be here forever. But I didn't realize God was only lending them to us. To guide us, love us, then leave us. *(Beat.)* My daddy was perfect y'all. He raised two smart girls, not to take no shi—nothin', from nobody. When he'd tuck us in at night, he'd always remind us: "This world may acknowledge your skin before they see your potential, but *never*…"

BANEATTA and BEVERLY. "Let them steal your magic."

Beverly and Baneatta catch eyes.

BEVERLY. Now, I don't wanna ruffle no church feathers, but Daddy revealed a family secret to *me* that I can't possibly hold in any longer. I just gotta say it. Y'all ready? *(Long beat.)* I, was his favorite—

BANEATTA. I'ma choke her!

SIMONE. Ma—

BEVERLY. He confided in me—

KENNY. This is better than *Drag Race*—

BEVERLY. Now Daddy, I wish I could sing you this song on my heart—

LOGAN. She sings?

KENNY. Like a tone-deaf dog—

BEVERLY. But I won't. I'll *save* it for the after-party.

> *Beverly reaches inside her purse, pulling out a small bottle of Hennessey.*

DADDY! (Beat.) I love being your *favorite*, and I can't wait to see you again. In God's heavenly gates.

> *She pours a little right near the casket.*

SIMONE. Did she just?—

BEVERLY. That's for *you*, Daddy! Thank y'all—

> *Beverly makes her way back to her seat. Reginald rises to the pulpit.*

REGINALD. Uh, Deacon Rivers, can you grab a sweat rag and clean that up, please? *(Beat.)* I'muh…speechless. I dunno if I'ma make it through all these memories. Y'all are *killin'* me. Okay, who's next?

SIMONE. Ma, you ready?

BANEATTA. Not just yet, baby.

KENNY. Well, I guess we should go up now.

> *Kenny stands.*

LOGAN. *(Sharp.)* We? I barely made it in here. Absolutely not!

KENNY. You said you'd stand with me—

REGINALD. Oh look, here comes my only boy, Kenneth.

> *Kenny makes his way to the mic stand.*

It's all you son.

KENNY. *(At the stand.)* I'll try not to repeat what's already been said about B. But, he was as thoughtful and caring as everyone describes him to be. Never a dull moment, well only if he was snoring, and even *that* was an event. *(Beat.)* B loved the parts of me that so many people in this family still choose to ignore—

BANEATTA. He better not—

BEVERLY. He should—

KENNY. Simone wasn't lying when she said his words made you feel like a diamond in the rough. *(Beat.)* "Boy, people goin' laugh at you and try and break you down to make themselves feel tall. But remember, you already know who you are. They've got so far to go." *(Beat.)* I carry his words with me every day.

I was about…thirteen, when I caught the acting bug. B was more excited than me. Whether I was the lead down front, or a Jellicle cat blending in with the set, he never missed a show. I could spot that cough a mile away.

For my fifteenth birthday, B surprised me with a trip down to New York City to see *The Lion King*. I 'bout fainted. But during the show I looked over and he was knocked out cold. I'm talking that good sleep. That kind where your head is tilted so far back, a fly could land on your tongue, and you wouldn't know it, kinda sleep. But I didn't wake him, I just stared at 'em. He was peaceful. Just as peaceful as he is right now.

Now, you best believe at the curtain call, he woke up, leapt to his feet and clapped harder than everyone around us. "That was a good play boy, wasn't it? I like the antelopes. You gon' be Simba one day." Too funny. *(Long beat.)* I'm opening a show next month, and this'll be the first time I won't hear that cough from the audience. But I know you're looking down from the lights, and that's all I need. I love you B—

Kenny goes to speak, but can't. He takes his seat in the applause.

LA'TRICE. Oooh Mama, that was touching. Maybe Cousin Kenny can spit an intro on my mixtape.

Kenny sits.

LOGAN. Kenny, that was gorgeous. I—

Kenny puts up his hand, stopping Logan from speaking.

REGINALD. Woof, it's gettin' misty in here.

BANEATTA. Well…I guess it's my turn.

Baneatta rises.

SIMONE. I can go up with you.

BANEATTA. No baby, I got this.

Baneatta makes her way to the mic.

REGINALD. And, here she is. My beautiful wife, and your new first lady, Mrs. Baneatta Mabry. Y'all give her a welcoming hand praise as she closes out our family remarks. Take your time now.

The congregation claps.

BANEATTA. Thank you all for being here today. This church has been the foundation of our family since I can remember. I can't recall a Sunday morning when Mama and Daddy weren't dragging us here in our sundresses, and propping us right there on that bench for service—

BEVERLY. Them ugly dresses.

BANEATTA. Just two years ago, Daddy's doctor called us and said his end was near. He said to say goodbye 'cause Daddy only had three months left. My heart shattered. Every time I tried to pray, I'd just break down. I could barely talk to God, let alone anyone else.

But when I finally found the strength to pray, God heard my prayer. That doctor's three-month diagnosis for Daddy turned into two more years of livin'. So, you can't tell me no doctor's chart has anything on God's final say.

The congregation responds in joy.

I can't pinpoint one specific memory, 'cause every day with you, Daddy, *was* a memory. Today, I'm cherishing those two extra years you gave us. It's just like you to pass when *you* want, with nobody around, sweetly in your sleep. But I guess God was finally ready to call you home.

No, you weren't perfect, but you loved us perfectly. *(Beat.)* Give Mama the biggest squeeze for me. *We* may've lost you, but I know she's mighty happy to see you. Bless y'all.

Baneatta sits, Reginald stands.

REGINALD. My Lord, my Lord. I dunno if I can follow all of y'all, but I'ma do my best, amen?

ALL. *(Ad-libs.)* Amen. / Yes, suh.

LA'TRICE. Ma, you got a peppermint or somethin'?—

REGINALD. Now, I met Brother Bernard before I even met Baneatta. I had just joined the deacon board here at St. Luke's, and he welcomed me with a handshake so firm, I think my hand still hurts.

Reginald laughs at his own joke.

LA'TRICE. God, I hope Uncle Reggie knows where this sermon is going—

BEVERLY. He don't—

REGINALD. Bernard had this eye twitch that made you sweat in your boots. You didn't know if he was gonna hug you, or slap you—

LOGAN. AMEN!

All eyes snap to Logan.

REGINALD. Now, he taught *me* the best way to keep a congregation is to hit 'em with a one-two punch. So, I'm gonna read *one* scripture, speak a few words of encouragement and get us on to the repast. Amen?—

ALL. Amen.

REGINALD. Now, let us open our Bibles to 2nd Corinthians, chapter 4, verses 17 and 18.

LOGAN. Where's Corinthians? Is this in alphabetical order?—

REGINALD. Verse 17 says, "For our light and momentary troubles are achieving for us an eternal glory that far outweighs them all." Verse 18 says, "So we fix our eyes not on what is seen, but on what is unseen, since what is seen is temporary, but what is unseen is eternal."

Whoo Lord, I felt that in my spirit. Lemme repeat that—

BEVERLY. PLEASE DON'T!

REGINALD. "For *OUR* light and momentary troubles" /

LA'TRICE. Uggh—

REGINALD. "Are *achieving* for us an *eternal* glory! So, we fix our eyes not on what is *seen*, but on what is *unseen*, since what is *seen* is temporary, but what is *unseen* is eternal."

I'ma let y'all *ruminate* on that, we'll swing on back. Now, let's quickly hop over to the book of John—

LOGAN. Does John have a last name?—

BEVERLY. He lied, he said *one* verse—

REGINALD. Chapter 14, verses 1 and 2!

LOGAN. Where are you, John?

REGINALD. It says, "Do not let your hearts be troubled. You believe in God; believe also in me." Verse 2 says, "My Father's house has many rooms; if that were not so, would I have told you that I am going there to prepare a place for you?"

LA'TRICE. Does this place have a fridge?—

REGINALD. See there, *Jesus* has already promised us a prepared place. Lemme here y'all say that, A PREPARED—

> *Reginald invites the audience to join.*

ALL and AUDIENCE. PLACE—

REGINALD. That's right! Which means when you check into the "Heavenly Gates *Motel*" your bellman can waltz that luggage straight on up to the *holy* suite; 'cause God done already prepaid your entire stay. The *WORD* says he's promised us a PREPARED— WHAT?!—

> *Reginald invites the audience again.*

ALL and AUDIENCE. PLACE—

REGINALD. Oh-yes. Now, Corinthians 4:17 reminds us that our troubles on this here earth are *momentary*. Lemme hear y'all say that:

ALL. Momentary!

REGINALD. AMEN! Meaning they won't last forever—

LA'TRICE. Like this sermon?—

REGINALD. See, in his final months of life, Bernard held the most precarious smile. I'd whisper to Baneatta: "Why is he smilin' so big, ain't he in pain?" I couldn't trust it. But y'all, *I-I-I* had forgotten what 2nd Corinthians 4:18 has taught us—

LOGAN. I too, forget—

> *Logan is still looking through his Bible.*

REGINALD. We must "fix our eyes not on what is seen, but on what *is*…"

ALL. UNSEEN! /

BANEATTA. Come on now!—

REGINALD. *(Beginning to sing it.)* See, *my* eyes were fixated on Bernard's body. But *Bernard's* eyes could already see his room in the sky. *Bernaarrd's* eyes could see God's PREPARED—

Reginald invites the congregation to join in.

ALL. *(Weaker than before.)* PLACE!

REGINALD. Oh, don't fall asleep on me now, we just gettin' jiggy wit it. I need y'all to get louder for Jesus: Bernard could see God's-PREPARED-what?—

ALL. PLACE!

Organ begins to rumble underneath.

REGINALD. Yes, suh. See when you *know* where you're going, you can *smile* right where you are! *(Beat.)* I dunno if y'all heard me the first time—

BEVERLY. WE DID!—

REGINALD. WHEN YOU *KNOW* WHERE-YOU-ARE-GOING, YOU CAN *SMILE. RIGHT-WHERE-YOU—*

Reginald invites the congregation to join in.

ALL. ARE!

The congregation erupts. Reginald speak-sings this next section. He's feelin' himself! The full company is to ad-lib responsibly through this entire upcoming section.

REGINALD. *Ouuuuur* Bernard's body, might be *lifeless* in this here earthly casket. But *I* know, that *I* know, that *you* know, that *I* know, he's dancin' above us right now!

SIMONE. Preach, Daddy!

REGINALD. In heaven!

Ad-libs/organ fill.

Beyond the gates!

Ad-libs/organ fill.

He's checked in his room.
> *Ad-libs/organ fill.*

And *he's* safe—

BANEATTA. Here he goes! /
> *Ad-libs/organ fill.*

REGINALD. He's got central air.
> *Ad-libs/organ fill.*

His bed's prepared.
> *Ad-libs/organ fill.*

He had to leave us.
> *Ad-libs/organ fill.*

To meet God there.
> *Ad-libs/organ fill.*

No more tumors.
> *Ad-libs/organ fill.*

No more tears.
> *Ad-libs/organ fill.*

Eternity!
> *Ad-libs/organ fill.*

For *alll* his years!
> *Ad-libs/organ fill.*

He's got a Jacuzzi.
> *Ad-libs/organ fill.*

Plus free cable.
> *Ad-libs/organ fill.*

See *MY* God.
> *Ad-libs/organ fill.*

He's able.
> *Ad-libs/organ fill.*

Bernard's sippin'.
> *Ad-libs/organ fill.*

He's up there dippin'.
> *Ad-libs/organ fill.*

He ordered chicken and biscuits!
> *Ad-libs/organ fill.*

From God's kitchen.
> *Ad-libs/organ fill.*

He's havin' seconds.
> *Ad-libs/organ fill.*

He's havin' thirds.
> *Ad-libs/organ fill.*

I know he's good.
> *Ad-libs/organ fill.*

It's in God's Word.
> *Ad-libs/organ fill.*

He's in his robe.
> *Ad-libs/organ fill.*

Toes all out.
> *Ad-libs/organ fill.*

If you want your room.
> *Ad-libs/organ fill.*

Give God a shout.
> *Ad-libs/organ fill.*

Say, "Yes, Lawd!"

ALL. Yes, Lawd!
> *Ad-libs/organ fill.*

REGINALD. YESSSSS, LAWD! Say, "YES, LAWWD!"

ALL. Yes, Lawd!
> *Ad-libs/organ fill.*

REGINALD. Yes, Lawd! HALLELUJAH!

> *The organ explodes with joy. The whole family is on their feet applauding. Logan joins. The roar of the crowd subsides.*

Now, I say all *that* to say this.

> *The full company collectively sighs and sits.*

Brother Bernard, thank you for teaching me everything I need to lead. Now, it's your time to rest. For you have served this family, and house of prayer with *full* commitment; earning your place in the everlasting. *(Beat.)* Bernard *Jenkins*, thank you for reminding us all to look up. Towards our *room*, in the sky!

> *One final organ lick. The church erupts with one final praise. Reginald wipes his head with a sweat rag.*

SIMONE. Daddy did that!

BANEATTA. He sure did. Now, hopefully we can sleep.

REGINALD. Well, with that, it looks like our service has come to its close. But hasn't it been beautiful?

ALL. *(Ad-libs.)* Yes it has. / Yes! / And long—

LOGAN. MAZEL TOV.

REGINALD. Oh…but before I say our final prayer, have I missed anybody? Anyone with final remarks?

> *Reginald looks out over the congregation. He sees no one.*

Great!… OH…

> *Suddenly, Brianna Jenkins makes her way to the mic.*

It seems I may've missed someone. I'm…I'm sorry ma'am, I don't know your name, but come on up. All are welcomed.

> *Brianna gets to the mic, she takes a moment to speak.*

BRIANNA. Hello. *(Beat.)* Good afternoon, everyone.

> *Congregation responds.*

I wish…I…knew more of you personally. But I…I don't. Uhh, I've driven a long ways to be here and I almost didn't come inside, but my heart convinced me it was the right thing to do. So, here I am. *(Beat.)* I'm Brianna. Brianna *Jenkins*. *(Long beat.)* Bernard's…other daughter.

BEVERLY. DA FUCK! Who is this?

LA'TRICE. MA, LANGUAGE!

BEVERLY. Other daughter, my ass—

SIMONE. Ma, do you know this woman?

Baneatta is frozen.

BRIANNA. I've been trying to get answers for years now.

LOGAN. Uh Kenny, does this always happen at Black funerals too?—

BRIANNA. I'm tired of being ignored—

KENNY. No, but *somebody* knows somethin'—

SIMONE. Ma, what should we do?

REGINALD. I uh…I'm sorry…uh /

BRIANNA. This may be a shock to some of you—

BEVERLY. Hold my purse, La'Trice! /

LA'TRICE. MA, DON'T!—

BRIANNA. But it's not to all of you /

SIMONE. SAY SOMETHIN'!

Beverly stands up from her seat.

BEVERLY. *(Screaming.)* MISS THANG, get *off* the mic before I *take* you off the mic!

BRIANNA. I deserve answers!

BEVERLY. Oh, I'll give you some.

REGINALD. Settle down now! /

LOGAN. Kenny, I can't watch this. I'll be outside—

KENNY. Logan, wai—

Logan runs out of the chapel.

BRIANNA. I'm sorry, I just /

LA'TRICE. MA! /

La'Trice tries to hold Beverly back.

BEVERLY. GET OFF ME!

BRIANNA. Baneatta, tell them—

SIMONE. You know her?!—

LA'TRICE. WorldStar!

Beverly pushes her way out of the pew. Reginald steps from behind the pulpit to protect Brianna from Beverly.

BEVERLY. HOW DARE YOU COME UP IN THIS CHURCH LYIN' ON MY DADDY!

Beverly charges towards Brianna. BLACKOUT!

When the lights restore, chaos ensues in strobe light/slow motion. Screams are heard as Simone, Kenny, and Reginald try to keep Beverly from reaching Brianna. Baneatta is silent, frozen in spotlight.

La'Trice realizes this is a prime opportunity for a performance. She steps to the mic, making the most of the moment amidst the madness.

LA'TRICE. *(Singing.)*
HOMIE'S PARADISE. HOMIE'S PARADISE.
HOMIE'S PARADISE. HOMIE'S PARADISE.
KOOL-AID WITH A LITTLE ICE, IN HOMIE'S PARADISE.
WE GON' BE ALRIGHT, IN HOMIE'S PARADISE.

The chaos eventually clears, leaving La'Trice at the mic. As the lights dim on her, they rise on Kenny and Simone in the kitchen.

KENNY. Did you know about this?

SIMONE. Do I *look* like I knew about this?

KENNY. I dunno, I thought since you and Ma are "so close" she would've at least told you—

SIMONE. Well, she didn't. B and I were "so close" and he didn't either.

KENNY. Like, how did this happen?

SIMONE. I think we both know *how*, it happened—

KENNY. Was B gettin' it in at the church?

SIMONE. Speaking of church! I saw your *thespian* friend run out the chapel when things got hot. Is he *okaaay*, or is dipping out a theme in the relationship?

KENNY. *(Beat.)* He's great, thanks for asking. But why you so concerned with us anyway? You and your mother have been completely rude to him all day, and you wonder why you don't hear from me—

SIMONE. Kenny, we've been through this, I support your lifestyle—

KENNY. MY IDENTITY, *not* my "lifestyle." A lifestyle is something you choose, my sexuality is who I am. Got it?

SIMONE. *(Beat.)* Yes, I apologize. Let me restate. I don't have any qualms with your *sexuality*, but it does trouble me that you can't find happiness within your own race—

KENNY. This again! /

SIMONE. Of all the men I've seen you date, none of them ever look like us—

KENNY. But, you *only* date Black men and yet you're still sing—

Kenny stops himself.

SIMONE. Si… Si?

KENNY. Si…

SIMONE. Single. Go-head say it, Kenny… *SINGLE!*—

KENNY. That came out wrong—

SIMONE. No, it didn't…it's the truth.

The two sit in silence for a moment.

KENNY. For the record, I *have* dated Black men, just not long enough for you to meet one. *(Beat.)* Growing up in our house everybody clung to their Bibles, but *I* clung to the closet. I was terrified of the truth. Like, how do you find yourself while trying to hide yourself? And from my closet door all I could hear was "It's a sin!" "*You're* a sin." Every Sunday morning it rang out like a hymn. So, when the church let me down, the closet kept me alive.

Logan was the first man to knock on my closet door and hug me instead of shame me. It wasn't his skin, it was his love. Yeah, he's super white and weird, but he makes your brother real happy. For the first time in my life I don't feel like a sin. My love for him is not a sin. So, *please* find a way to be happy for me. Just, this, once. *(Long beat.)* And since we're on the topic of men, you wanna tell me what happened with Derrick?—

SIMONE. I don't.

KENNY. I tried.

SIMONE. *(Long beat.)* Derrick was obsessed with my body, but intimidated by my mind, it was exhausting. He wanted arm candy and I'ma whole damn candy bar. The more I demanded of him, the less he gave. I suggested therapy, he said no. I did everything Mommy told me to do, but nothing worked. My love was never enough. So, instead of talking to me... *(Beat.)* He cheated—

KENNY. Oh my God, Simone. / I

SIMONE. I cracked. I couldn't process it. My body went into shock and I shut down. *(Beat.)* I...stopped eating. For three straight months /

KENNY. WHAT?! /

SIMONE. He disappeared and so did my appetite. *(Beat.)* So there, that's why I'm so frail—

KENNY. Why didn't you / call?

SIMONE. *(Losing it.)* Derrick was the husband I prayed for. I could see him waiting at the altar when I walked down the aisle. Elegant, on Daddy's arm. I saw our children, our home, our future, just steps ahead of me... *(Beat.)* But, we never even made it to the church. I'm an embarrassment to this family—

KENNY. No, you aren't /

SIMONE. Sometimes, I put on my wedding dress to see what it would've felt like. I lost myself in him, and nothing's left. *(Beat.)* I can't seem to understand why God would want me to hurt this way.

KENNY. Simone, come here /

SIMONE. *(Breaking down.)* No, I'm fine. I promise, I'm good now. I-I-I'm fine. /

KENNY. SIMONE!

SIMONE. I just needed a moment...but I can hold it together /

KENNY. You don't have to /

SIMONE. I can. I'm okay. I promise. Everything's okay. I'm okay—

Simone repeats herself until Kenny hugs her, calming her down.

KENNY. It's alright, let it out. I got you. Just *breathe*...one big deep breath now.

They breathe together.

There you go. *(Beat.)* Simone?

SIMONE. Yeah?

KENNY. Let's get one thing straight, okay? *(Beat.)* You always been a whole damn candy bar, girl. I had to grow up with it.

SIMONE. Shut up—

KENNY. But you taught me strength. Maybe I don't tell you enough, but hear me now. Your strength never came from no man. You had it long before you met Derrick and it's still right here. You got that?

SIMONE. I'm listenin'.

KENNY. So, don't let his raggedy ass deprive you of your joy, girl. Let him have Little White Riding Hood, 'cause quiet as it's kept he was…nope—

Kenny stops himself.

SIMONE. He was what?! Aun-aun don't do that Kenny, say it…

Kenny stalls for a moment.

KENNY. He…umm… *Sis*…he had a busted face.

SIMONE. OH MY GOD! Aunty said the same thing. Why ain't nobody tell *me*?

KENNY. What could we say? It was your heart, and his…

SIMONE and KENNY. Face.

KENNY. *(Channeling his inner preacher.)* But he's gone now! He don't matter no more. What *matters* is us, we gotta do better—

SIMONE. *(Beat.)* We do.

KENNY. So, starting today, when you're struggling you call me immediately. That sibling rivalry shit ends with Ma and Aunt Bev. I'm your brother, girl. This all we got, let's use it.

SIMONE. I'm down. *(Beat.)* And I'll uh…apologize to Logan. Since the breakup, it's been real hard for me not to see red when I see white people—

KENNY. I get it, but he's actually been the one telling me to call you. He never wants our relationship to pull me away from my family. So, maybe give him a shot?

SIMONE. I'll give 'em, one.

KENNY. That's a start.

> *They hear Mother Jones.*

Oh no!   SIMONE. DEAR GOD!

SIMONE. Is Mother Jones still singing "Amazing Grace"?

KENNY. No, "Amazing Grace" is singing Mother Jones. Let's find Daddy.

SIMONE. Yeah, let's go. Help her Lord!

KENNY. No, help us!

> *Lights rise on Logan frantically pacing St. Luke's Church steps. He's hitting his weed pen while on the phone with his mother. He takes a hit.*

LOGAN. Yeah, you were *right*, Mom, I should've sent the Bundt cake. *(Listening beat.)* Of course I'm the only white person here, and half the church stares at me like I took a *shit* on the cross. *(Listening beat.)* THIS *IS* CALM!

> *Logan takes another hit. He doesn't realize that La'Trice has emerged and is watching him from the top of the stairs.*

Mom, this was supposed to be the day. I was going to ask his father if I could propose, but from the moment we got off the train, I just lost my cool. She shipoopied away. Like, bye girl. Have a good trip. Miss you, mean it.

> *Logan takes another hit.*

I wanted to be his crutch today, but instead we've been bickering. It's his mother. She's like a wedge between us. *(Beat.)* She'll never accept me. No matter what I do. No matter how much I love him—

LA'TRICE. HIII, LUCAS—

LOGAN. SHIT, I gotta go. *(Listening beat.)* Yeah, yeah I will. Yep. 'Kay, love you too. Bye.

> *Logan hangs up, pockets his weed pen, and turns around.*

Hiiii, La'Trice! Like, exactly how long have you been standing there?

LA'TRICE. What's in that pen?—

LOGAN. So, that was my mother. She just wanted an update—

LA'TRICE. The pen—

LOGAN. Where is everyone?

LA'TRICE. What's in it?

LOGAN. Where's *your* mother?

LA'TRICE. I want some—

LOGAN. We should head back inside—

LA'TRICE. Don't *even* try to play me, Lucas—

LOGAN. *LOGAN* CALEB LEIBOWITZ IS MY EQUITY NAME! She's very Jewish, but I love her. Why is it impossible for *anyone* in this family to remember it?

LA'TRICE. *(Screaming.)* WHO YOU SCREAMIN' AT THO? I'm just trying to have a civilized adult conversation as the *sixteen*-year-old I'm 'bout to be.

LOGAN. *(Beat.)* Forgive me. I—…this is honestly the most bizarre funeral I've ever attended—

LA'TRICE. Man, this is tame, but it did get a little wild in there—

LOGAN. A little?! *(Beat.)* Your mother, who's fabulous by the way, almost Jerry Springered that poor woman. Did she survive?—

LA'TRICE. Yeeeaaah, she aight. Ma didn't get to her. But when Uncle Reggie pulled Ma back, she fought him a little *too* hard and her right nipple ring popped out—

LOGAN. Oh dear—

LA'TRICE. I told her *not* to wear that bra in public, but she don't listen to nobody but Oprah.

LOGAN. *(Beat.)* Where's Kenny?

LA'TRICE. He in there somewhere. I needed a moment away from the crazies—

LOGAN. Amen! *(Beat.)* I should go find him.

Logan steps to go inside.

LA'TRICE. So…you Kenny boyfriend?

LOGAN. *(Long beat.)* Ummm…we should—

LA'TRICE. While you was updating your mama, I feel like I heard you say you wanna *propose*. *(Long beat.)* Are you gon' do it?

LOGAN. You ask a lot of questions—

LA'TRICE. And they *all* deserve answers. Are, you, gon' do it?

LOGAN. I…I'd like to. I have the ring, *(Beat.)* but I need his parents' blessing.

LA'TRICE. Woof, good luck with dat! Aunty Baneatta is a tough cookie. Why you think I kept askin' "Who is this white boy?" I wasn't askin' 'cause I care. I was askin' 'cause I wanted somebody to acknowledge you.

> *Logan hugs La'Trice. He's squeezing her tight and won't let go. He's emotional.*

LOGAN. *(Weepy.)* How thoughtful of you. Oh, my, God. That's the sweetest thing I've heard all day—

LA'TRICE. Uh…Loogaan. I know we *kinda* family, but like get off of me—

> *Logan lets go.*

LOGAN. Yeah, sorry! It's just been a day. And Baneatta's made it crystal clear that I'm *not* welcomed here. So, it's nice to hear that someone thinks I am. *(Beat.)* Thank you, La'Trice.

> *Logan goes to hug La'Trice again, but settles for an awkward high five instead.*

LA'TRICE. No sweat yo, fam is fam. *(Beat.)* And I say propose. You ain't never gon' get the approval you want anyway, so go be like Nike: "Just Do It!"

LOGAN. *(Chuckling.)* I'll consider that. Thanks for the advice.

LA'TRICE. Anytime *Logan*, I got you, bruh. *(Beat.)* But like uh… do you got *me*?

LOGAN. What? Got you, how?

LA'TRICE. Puff puff pass—

LOGAN. I don't know what you're talking about—

LA'TRICE. Yes you do *Nigga*, I could smell it from the steps—

LOGAN. NO! No, way. You are underag—ABSOLUTELY NOT! And if you open your mouth to Kenny I—

LA'TRICE. You'll-You'll-You'll—   LOGAN. I'll-I'll-I'll—
You'll *what*?

LOGAN. Just please don't!

LA'TRICE. I won't.

LOGAN. THANK YOU /

LA'TRICE. Tell *Kenny* nothin'. Though I guess I could though, huh? But I don't wanna *have* to. Ya feel me?

LOGAN. Are you blackmailing me right now?

LA'TRICE. I'm a Black woman.

> *La'Trice and Logan stare off. Logan is perplexed. La'Trice extends her hand. After a moment, Logan pulls out his weed pen.*

LOGAN. One hit, and this never happened—

LA'TRICE. Fall back, Lulu Lemon, I'm a professional.

> *As La'Trice takes a hit, the lights fade on them and rise on Baneatta, Beverly, and Brianna in the pastor's study. Brianna is seated, as is Baneatta, who's still silent. Beverly paces back and forth. We sit in silence for a second, and then:*

BEVERLY. Well, I guess I should start this conversation off with an apology. Ummm, what's your name again?—

BRIANNA. *(Firm.)* Brianna—

BEVERLY. Yeah! *Brianna*, I knew that. *Brianna*, please excuse my ratchet actions in the sanctuary. That was definitely not how Daddy raised us to behave in the house of the Lort—

BRIANNA. It's fine /

BEVERLY. No, it ain't. I let my emotions get the best of me, and that was wrong. *(Beat.)* Oh and uh, contrary to the church chatter, I was *not* about to rip your wig off. I just wanted a closer look—

BRIANNA. I know you weren't and it's not a wig!

BEVERLY. *Oooh*, good for you girl.

> *Baneatta sucks her teeth.*

Somethin' in your teeth, *Baneatta*? Keep rollin' them eyes, I hope they get stuck in the back of ya head—

BRIANNA. I feel like a fool for ruining his service—

BEVERLY. Oh no, there's only *one* fool in this room and it ain't you—

BRIANNA. Please, no fighting. I just want answers—

BEVERLY. Well, perhaps *Baneatta* can enlighten us, since she's been sitting on the truth for God knows how long—

BANEATTA. ENOUGH! *(Beat.)* Yes…I knew about Brianna /

BEVERLY. But you failed to tell the rest of the family?!

BANEATTA. I WAS PROTECTING THE FAMILY! Something you don't know how to do, Bever—

BRIANNA. PLEASE stop screaming /

BEVERLY. *(Snapping.)* YOU DON'T HAVE TO PROTECT *SHIT* FOR ME!

BRIANNA. STOP IT!

BEVERLY. Sorry.

> *The room is thick and silent again.*

BANEATTA. I went straight to Daddy when you first emailed me. I asked him about you, but he wouldn't answer me; he couldn't even look in my direction. But, when I mentioned your mother's name… his eyes said it all.

BEVERLY. Who's your mama?

BRIANNA. Her name, *was* Evelyn. Evelyn Simmons. I was raised in Alabama. But born in Raleigh. Ain't that where y'all originally from?

BANEATTA. Sure are.   BEVERLY. Yeah.

BEVERLY. I was the only born up *North*. Baneatta was born down in Raleigh. Our mama was pregnant with me when Daddy's company relocated to New Haven, so they raised us here. Now, how old are you?

BANEATTA. Don't—

BRIANNA. Forty-four.

BEVERLY. *(Beat.)* Forty-four? OH-MY GOD. Why didn't you tell me?—

BRIANNA. Tell her what? What is it?

> *No one answers.*

Somebody talk to me—

BANEATTA. Beverly is forty-four. *(Beat.)* That's why I didn't tell you. I knew it would hurt you.

> *A thick beat. Then:*

BRIANNA. My mother gave me your last name, but wouldn't murmur a word about my father. Ooh, she loathed me. I think every time she looked in my eyes, she saw him, her mistake. She dealt with me, but never *loved* me, so we weren't very close. For all I knew, my daddy was already in the ground or behind bars somewhere. And I begged and begged her to tell me more about him, but her shame kept her secret.

A couple weeks before she passed, she finally gave me his first name, but nothin' else. Ya know, there are a lot of Bernard Jenkins in this world. I didn't know where to begin. *(Beat.)* At her funeral, I looked out over the congregation and realized I had no one. She was my only family, and she was gone.

So, when I finally found y'all I was so excited not to be alone anymore. But you, just like my mama, kept my daddy from me. *(Beat.)* Now, he's gone too—

BANEATTA. When Daddy got sick, I couldn't bring you up—

BEVERLY. And exactly how long *did* you know about Brianna. *Baneatta?*—

BRIANNA. Three years—

BEVERLY. THREE YEARS?! THREE WHOLE YEARS and you ain't tell a soul—

BANEATTA. I couldn't—

BEVERLY. WHY NOT?! You seem to be able to do everything else with your tenure and your cars and your degrees, right?—

BANEATTA. You don't understand—

BEVERLY. OH, I THINK I DO. You lie to yourself 'til your lies are the truth.

BANEATTA. I HAD TO!

Reginald knocks on the door and swings in.

REGINALD. Sorry to interrupt, but we should head over to the burial ground. Folks are gettin' anxious. Can we continue this conversation at the repast?

BEVERLY. We need one more minute.

REGINALD. Alright. *(Beat.)* I'm glad to see no one's being *tackled*—

BANEATTA. *Reginald!*

REGINALD. That's my cue.

> *Reginald exits. Baneatta takes a moment to speak. These words are heavy for her.*

BANEATTA. We didn't leave Raleigh 'cause Daddy got a new job. We left, 'cause if we didn't, Mama was leavin' Daddy. Beverly, you weren't born up North. Y'all were born just months apart and everybody knew you two had the same daddy, 'cept Mama was married to him. I had never seen her cry like that. The screaming and fighting, it never ended. "Bernard, it's her or us," she said. And Daddy chose us. So, we left North Carolina, but even at four years old, I knew why.

I kept askin' them about you. About my *other* sister, but nobody wanted to talk about it. *(Beat.)* One day, Mama grabbed me by my jaw: "*Stop askin*," she said. "That girl ain't your blood. Every time you speak her name you betray this family." So, I stopped. *(Beat.)* Forty years later you pop up outta nowhere. Asking questions I couldn't answer. What was I supposed to do? It wasn't my story to tell. I wanted you to meet Daddy, trust me, I did. But I promised Mama I'd bury it, for the family. If I could go back and change it, I would…but I can't. *(Beat.)* I'm sorry, Brianna. Please forgive me. *(Beat.)* I'm so sorry.

> *Baneatta almost breaks. Beverly tries to console her, but Baneatta stops her. The sisters sit in silence.*

BRIANNA. When I pulled into that church parking lot, I was fuming with rage. But, as I sat in that back pew, and took in your stories, *love* began to wash over me, and I felt compelled to speak. But when I finally mustered up the courage…Beverly 'bout killed me—

BEVERLY. Girl, I didn't know who you were /

BRIANNA. No, no, no, girl. I get it. *(Long beat.)* It seems to me like we all been carrying everybody else's weight.

BEVERLY. The women always do.

BANEATTA. Amen.

BRIANNA. But I think, there's been much more love here all along.

You two can't see it, but y'all are the perfect pair. Two dynamic Black women. You wear it in different ways, but both are fabulous—

BEVERLY. Don't I know it.

BRIANNA. And you love each other tremendously. I want some of that love.

BEVERLY. And you'll get it. *(Beat.)* Baneatta, you should've told me. You didn't have to carry that burden alone for all these years and how *dare* Mama make you. That's the problem with church folk, our mindsets. We always protectin' our mess to put on our best. For WHO?! Can't he see it all, anyway? Shi—shoot, it pisses me off. You deserved to know Daddy, and we shoulda known you long ago. *(Beat.)* You know what?! We startin' anew. We gotta let all that mess go. Stand up!

BANEATTA. Excuse me?

BEVERLY. You heard me. We shakin' off the past. You ain't carrying it no mo'—

BANEATTA. Beverly—

BEVERLY. Brianna, you ready?

BRIANNA. I'm nervous.

BEVERLY. Don't be, I'ma teach you how to Dougie. Now, I know up here in New Haven y'all like to keep it stiff and together. But down at Ebenezer Baptist Church of Christ Disciples of Christ Atlanta branch incorporated, we get *messy*. When you been holdin' on to something too long, and God's ready for you to release it. There's only one way to do it.

BRIANNA. And what's that?

Beverly physicalizes this as she demonstrates.

BEVERLY. HUH-HA-HALLELUJAH!

BRIANNA. Oh-my.

BEVERLY. Don't knock it 'til you try it.

BANEATTA. I ain't trying that.

BEVERLY. Well, you missin' out. Come on Brianna, get into it. On three.

BRIANNA. I dunno—

BEVERLY. One, two, three.

> *Beverly and Brianna do it together.*

BRIANNA and BEVERLY. HUH-HA-HALLELUJAH!

BEVERLY. That's it! How you feel?

BRIANNA. My back. Girl, my back ain't gon' make it—

BEVERLY. Yes, it will. Trust Jesus. Baneatta, come on now. We gettin' free on three. One, two, three.

BRIANNA and BEVERLY. HUH-HA-HALLELUJAH! HUH-HA-HALLELUJAH! HUH-HA-HALLELUJAH!

BEVERLY. Come on Baneatta, free yourself.

BRIANNA and BEVERLY. HUH-HA-HALLELUJAH!

> *Somehow the two get lost in it. To Beverly's surprise, Brianna begins to enjoy it. The actresses are to repeat this as long as they need. Laughter is added. The two continue the chant, dancing and bonding. Baneatta remains tentative, but has stood to her feet. As their chant becomes more joyous, something in Baneatta shifts. Witnessing their fellowship ignites something in her. She mumbles her way into the chant without them noticing.*

BEVERLY, BRIANNA, and BANEATTA. HUH-HA-HALLELUJAH! HUH-HA-HALLELUJAH! HUH-HA-HALLELUJAH!

> *The sisters continue. Slowly and unexpectedly, Baneatta's chant explodes in a spiritual release. Her voice bellows as her hands extend to the sky. Tears fall from her eyes. She's so overcome with release her volume begins to overpower theirs. Beverly and Brianna stop and turn to witness Baneatta's breakthrough. They're shocked into silence.*

BANEATTA. HUH-HA-HALLELUJAH! HUH-HA-HALLELUJAH! HALLELUJAH! HALLELUJAH! HALLELUJAH! HALLELUJAH! I RELEASE IT. HALLELUJAH! I RELEASE ITTTTTTT.

> *Finally, she's free. After a moment of peace, Baneatta opens her eyes.*

BEVERLY. How you feelin'?

BANEATTA. Free… Finally, free.

BRIANNA. Me too. Though my back, chile. I'm out.

Brianna takes a seat.

BANEATTA. Wow, thank you for that, Beverly.

BEVERLY. Don't thank me, thank God. *(Beat.)* He knew we needed this.

BRIANNA and BANEATTA. We did.

The three sisters take each other in.

BANEATTA. Well, I think we're past our minute. We should head on out.

BRIANNA. Yes, let's.

BANEATTA. But Brianna, leave your car here at the church. You're riding with us—

BRIANNA. Oh no, I don't have to—

BANEATTA. Yes-you-do. You're family.

BRIANNA. Really?

BEVERLY. You sure are! Though, I'm sittin' in the front seat.

BANEATTA. Get used to that.

BRIANNA. Oh, I got it.

BANEATTA. Good!

BEVERLY. *(Beat.)* Alright now, sistas. Let's go bury our daddy.

As the lights dim, the three sisters take one big deep breath together. A song like Mahalia Jackson's "Take My Hand, Precious Lord" smoothens our transition.*

When lights rise again, we are in the church banquet hall at the repast. A long dinner table is covered by a white table cloth center stage. Chicken and biscuits are spread throughout the table. The family hasn't started eating, but La'Trice has, 'cause she's still high.

KENNY. Wow, La'Trice is *devouring* that chicken like she is—

LA'TRICE. *(Waving.)* HIIIIIII, Kenny and *Logan*!

LOGAN. Hi there!!!   KENNY. Hey.

KENNY. See, progress. She remembers your name.

---

* See Note on Songs/Recordings at the back of this volume.

LOGAN. I know, she's sweet. We had a moment.

KENNY. What kind of moment?

LA'TRICE. JUST DO IT!

KENNY. Just do what?

LOGAN. Sit, let's sit!

KENNY. *(Suspicious.)* Okay…

> *They sit.*

LOGAN. Fill me in, why chicken and biscuits?

KENNY. Oh, it's a B tradition. Always with a Dr. Pepper and a side of baked beans.

LOGAN. What about vegans and vegetarians?

KENNY. Good luck.

> *Simone interrupts.*

SIMONE. Thespians!… Sorry to interrupt.

KENNY. WHAT, MA?! DID YOU JUST CALL ME? Yep, I'll be right there!

> *Kenny leaves Logan and Simone alone.*

LOGAN. I assume this is a setup?

SIMONE. Perhaps. *(Beat.)* Umm…I uh, have some baggage that I'm still working through, and today I accidentally smacked you with a suitcase or two—

LOGAN. You're totally fine. I get—

SIMONE. Black woman speaking—

LOGAN. Zip.

SIMONE. Thank you! So…in short. *(Beat.)* I apologize. I see the way his smile lights up when he says your name. Plus, he had some *real* guts bringing you around our crazy family. It's like a reverse *Get Out*. I haven't met many of his…boyfriends, but I think he really wanted us to meet *you*. I guess that makes you one hell of a catch.

LOGAN. Oh my—Thank you, Simone. That's the second-sweetest thing said to me today—

> *Logan goes in for the stiff hug. Simone politely ducks it.*

SIMONE. Whoa whoa whoa whoa whoa now, slow it down. One step at a time.

LOGAN. Copy!

SIMONE. Oh, and if you break his heart or cheat on him, I'll snap your legs in three places and hide the bones. Just kidding… Hahahaha. But am I? Seriously, welcome to the family

Lights shift to Baneatta and Reginald.

REGINALD. Baneatta, that was beautiful.

BANEATTA. What you talkin' 'bout?

REGINALD. Having Brianna ride with us to the burial.

BANEATTA. It's the least I could do.

REGINALD. But you didn't have to, and you did.

Reginald kisses Baneatta on the cheek. Lights shift to La'Trice chompin' down as Simone and Brianna approach the table.

LA'TRICE. Oooh look, my new aunty!

BRIANNA. Oh hi, darlin'—

LA'TRICE. Did my mama apologize? She ratchet!—

BRIANNA. She did indeed, we're all good.

LA'TRICE. Thank God. *(Beat.)* You look nice. You dress classy. You rich?

SIMONE. La'Trice, we don't ask people that!

LA'TRICE. Why not? She family and I gotta birthday coming up.

BRIANNA. Darlin', I wish I was rich. Are you?

LA'TRICE. No, but *Homie's Paradise* gon' make me millions!

BRIANNA. She's a rapper?

SIMONE. Not quite.

Reginald claps to get everyone's attention.

REGINALD. Okay, alright now everybody, let's circle up before we dig into our meal.

LA'TRICE. Oops.

The family gathers. This monologue is meant to engage the entire audience.

REGINALD. Well…*what* a day. Y'all witnessed something quite… special in that sanctuary. *(Beat.)* Family, in its purest and most fragile form. We are all guilty of pretending our families are sparkle-proof knowing good and well, there's just one closet at home full of dust.

And Brother Bernard, you left us with…*some dust*. But we will heal and move forward. 'Cause that's what families do. Amen?

ALL. Amen!

REGINALD. Aye-men! Now, everybody eat up, then clean up, 'cause this house of the Lord has no maids—

BANEATTA. Uh, before we sit, may I say one last thing? /

LOGAN. I'm shvitzing /

BEVERLY. She just gotta have the last word!

REGINALD. Go'n right ahead, honey.

> *The banquet hall goes quiet. Suddenly, Baneatta makes her way over to Beverly, who is turned away from her, but turns back to say:*

BEVERLY. What do you—

> *Baneatta swiftly hugs Beverly long and tight. It feels like time has frozen. This hug means so much more than an apology. It echos sisterhood, pain, and loss all wrapped into one. No words are spoken, but tears fall. Finally, Baneatta lets go.*

BANEATTA. Church family, I would be remiss not to introduce you to our new sister. Who I made the mistake of hiding for way too long.

> *Baneatta points to Brianna.*

This beautiful woman is Brianna Jenkins.

BRIANNA. Hello everybody, it's a blessin' to be here.

BANEATTA. We got *a lot* of catchin' up to do, but I'm looking forward to it—

BEVERLY. Me too! Though I'm still the YOUNGEST!… *(Beat.)* I think…

> *Baneatta shifts her focus to Logan.*

BANEATTA. And I should also acknowledge…Kenny's—

A moment of silent tension.

KENNY. Partner—

BANEATTA. In *Christ*! Logan, thank you for being here with Kenneth to support the family. It says a lot.

LOGAN. Oh-my-gosh, thank *YOU*. That's the third-sweetest thing said to me today. I am truly /

Baneatta cuts him off.

BANEATTA. Okay baby, so church family that's the Mabry/Jenkins clan. Again, thank you for all your love. We feel it. *(Beat.)* And *Daddy*, we're eatin' your favorite meal today: chicken and biscuits. You couldn't cook it—

BEVERLY. Not at all!—

BANEATTA. But oooohhh you *sure* could eat it! *(Beat.)* We'll miss you, and we *love* you. Alright now, y'all eat up!

LA'TRICE. Finally!

ALL. Let's go. / Amen. / Okay!

The murmurings finally take the family to the table. As they sit, the picture from stage left to right is: Logan, Kenny, Reginald, Baneatta, Brianna, Beverly, La'Trice, then Simone. They all fill their plates with chicken and biscuits.

BEVERLY. Simone, don't think I forgot about the club, girl. We still going!

SIMONE. No, we are not—

BEVERLY. *YES*, WE ARE!

SIMONE. No, we are not—

BEVERLY. We are! I done slipped some Hennessy in this church cup. *You* coming too.

BRIANNA. Oh-no, I'm not. My back is still recovering.

REGINALD. I love the woman I married. I'm mighty proud of her today.

BANEATTA. And I'm proud of my *pastor*. You'll have to show me "how proud" you are a little later—

REGINALD. Don't you start nothin' in God's house that we can't finish.

Reginald kisses Baneatta on the cheek as the church music swells. Everyone is feasting. There is joy, there is laughter, there is the fellowship that can only be felt in a Black church dining hall.

A voiceover of Mother Jones's not so "Amazing Grace" crescendos. The lights fade to black as we savor our last glimpse of this glowing family.

End of Play

PROPERTY LIST
(Use this space to create props lists for your production)

SOUND EFFECTS
(Use this space to create sound effects lists for your production)

Dear reader,

Thank you for supporting playwrights by purchasing this acting edition! You may not know that Dramatists Play Service was founded, in 1936, by the Dramatists Guild and a number of prominent play agents to protect the rights and interests of playwrights. To this day, we are still a small company committed to our partnership with the Guild, and by proxy all playwrights, established and aspiring, working in the English language.

Because of our status as a small, independent publisher, we respectfully reiterate that this text may not be distributed or copied in any way, or uploaded to any file-sharing sites, including ones you might think are private. Photocopying or electronically distributing books means both DPS and the playwright are not paid for the work, and that ultimately hurts playwrights everywhere, as our profits are shared with the Guild.

We also hope you want to perform this play! Plays are wonderful to read, but even better when seen. If you are interested in performing or producing the play, please be aware that performance rights must be obtained through Dramatists Play Service. This is true for *any* public performance, even if no one is getting paid or admission is not being charged. Again, playwrights often make their sole living from performance royalties, so performing plays without paying the royalty is ultimately a loss for a real writer.

This acting edition is the **only approved text for performance**. There may be other editions of the play available for sale from other publishers, but DPS has worked closely with the playwright to ensure this published text reflects their desired text of all future productions. If you have purchased a revised edition (sometimes referred to as other types of editions, like "Broadway Edition," or "[Year] Edition"), that is the only edition you may use for performance, unless explicitly stated in writing by Dramatists Play Service.

Finally, this script cannot be changed without written permission from Dramatists Play Service. If a production intends to change the script in any way—including casting against the writer's intentions for characters, removing or changing "bad" words, or making other cuts however small—without permission, they are breaking the law. And, perhaps more importantly, changing an artist's work. Please don't do that!

We are thrilled that this play has made it into your hands. We hope you love it as much as we do, and thank you for helping us keep the American theater alive and vital.

Note on Songs/Recordings, Images, or Other Production Design Elements

Be advised that Dramatists Play Service, Inc., neither holds the rights to nor grants permission to use any songs, recordings, images, or other design elements mentioned in the play. It is the responsibility of the producing theater/organization to obtain permission of the copyright owner(s) for any such use. Additional royalty fees may apply for the right to use copyrighted materials.

For any songs/recordings, images, or other design elements mentioned in the play, works in the public domain may be substituted. It is the producing theater/organization's responsibility to ensure the substituted work is indeed in the public domain. Dramatists Play Service, Inc., cannot advise as to whether or not a song/arrangement/recording, image, or other design element is in the public domain.